GW00692386

 know
the
game

Cycling

**Published in collaboration with the
CYCLISTS' TOURING CLUB**

CONTENTS

Page

INTRODUCTION 4

CYCLING EFFICIENCY 6

THE BICYCLE
Handlebars 7
Saddles 8
Frame design 9
Pedals 10
Gearing 11
Cycle chains 12
Variable gearing 12
Gear table 13
Hub gears 14
Derailleur gears 14
Wheels and tyres 16
Spokes 17
Hubs 17
Brakes 18
Brakes in use 20
Chain set 20

CARRYING LUGGAGE 21

Page

LIGHTING 22

BICYCLE MAINTENANCE 24
Bearings and adjustment 24
Lubrication 26
Care of your cycle 26
How to mend a puncture 26
Keep your bicycle in good order 28

SKILFUL CYCLING 29
The National Cycling Proficiency Scheme .. 30

CYCLING CLUBS 32

GROUP RIDING 32

CYCLE TOURING 33
Competition for cycle tourists 34

CYCLE SPORT 35
Time trialing 35
Track racing 37
Road racing 38
Road racing—affiliation and licences .. 40
Schoolboys' Championships 40

FOREWORD

What does cycling mean to you? A daily jaunt to school, to the office or the factory, an occasional trip to the shops, or a run out into the country with some pals? No matter how near home or how far afield your wheels may take you, here in "Know the Game—CYCLING," you will find something to increase your knowledge and widen your interest in this simplest yet most rewarding of all pastimes.

As with any other sport or recreation, however, cycling is a skill to be learned and practised properly, and real enjoyment of the game comes only to those who take the trouble to acquire the skill. It is more than just a matter of throwing a leg across a saddle and hoping for the best, or forgetting to grease the chain or pump the tyres from one month's end to the next. The right kind of bicycle, the correct riding position, thorough maintenance, a sound knowledge and use of equipment; all these are essential elements in "knowing the game."

For those with wider horizons, the unending pleasures of cycle-touring and the excitement of cycle-racing lie in store. This booklet will provide the key to a better knowledge and understanding of these finer points of the game, as well as explaining the benefits to be gained from belonging to such national bodies as the Cyclists' Touring Club—the oldest touring club in the world—and the organisations controlling the racing sport.

Cycling is a game that everyone, young and old, can enjoy. Here is how to enjoy it.

Manuel.

Secretary Cyclists' Touring Club

INTRODUCTION

The bicycle is so familiar that we don't often stop to think about what it does for us. Like the "Seven League Boots" of the fable, it enables us to cover ground much more speedily than we could running or walking and keep going at this pace for a considerable time.

The bicycle began in the form of an adults' toy early in the 19th century; a kind of scooter but with larger wheels. The rider sat on a frame that connected the two wheels together and propelled it along the ground with his feet; this was known as the "hobby horse". Later, the front wheel was provided with a hinge which allowed it to be steered. Eventually, in 1839, a Scot named Macmillan devised a method of driving the rear wheel by a system of levers and treadles (Fig. 1), and in 1842 he made an 80-mile journey

Fig. 1

in two days. Further development was rather slow until a Frenchman added pedals and cranks and thus produced the first "velocipede" or "boneshaker".

Lighter materials followed, and it was soon found that a larger driving wheel provided more leverage and drove the machine faster, so the front wheel increased in size with each new model until it appeared as the high bicycle popularly known as the "penny farthing". The size of the driving wheel was limited by the length of the rider's leg and the diameter of the wheel was used to indicate both the size of the cycle and the ratio of the gear. To the present day we still convert our gear ratios by a formula which shows the size of the wheel which would have been needed on a penny farthing to produce the same effect.

On this large-wheeled bicycle the rider was seated almost directly over the centre of the wheel. Consequently, any obstruction which stopped the front wheel tended to throw the rider over the handlebars. This drawback led to the introduction of the safety bicycle which we know today (Fig. 2).

Fig. 2

Though invented in 1879 the safety bicycle did not become popular until the "Rover" of 1885. This brought the wheel sizes down by providing chain drive to the rear wheel. The invention of the pneumatic tyre in 1888 by John Boyd Dunlop and later improvements have resulted in the present-day lightweight bicycle.

The bicycle has not, in the main, altered greatly during the last 70 years or so, although stronger materials have been introduced and weight reduced. Variable gears have been introduced and have proved a great help. Nowadays, multi-geared bicycles are quite common.

Wheel diameter has been standardised at 26 or 27 inches, but in the early sixties the Moulton appeared (with 16 inch wheels) and since then the "small-wheeler" with a compromise wheel size of 20 inches has become part of the cycling scene, with the accent on shopping and general use.

Twenty-inch-wheel bicycles have a quick adjustment of handlebar and saddle height over a large range, so that they can be used by all members of the family. Some machines of this type have a hinged frame, so that they can be folded and stowed away in the boot of a car.

Fig. 3
A 20 inch wheel bicycle

CYCLING EFFICIENCY

Cycling does not require great strength and if you take the trouble to learn how to pedal correctly you will find that it can be quite easy.

Efficient pedalling means more than just pushing the pedals down—it means turning them round. The ankle joints should be used as well as the knee and hip joints.

At the top of the stroke, the heel should be as low as possible and the toe ready to push the pedal forward by the straightening of the foot, whilst it is also being pushed down through the straightening of the leg. As the foot descends, the toe is pointed down so that the pedal can be pulled backwards.

Fig. 4

Then, as the pedal rises, the foot is lifted and the heel is dropped again ready for the next forward and downward push. The result of this is a smooth circular movement (Fig. 4) that can be kept up for a very long time. Why? Because it uses all the muscles in the legs and feet instead of a stiff climbing action that soon tires the thighs.

It is important that the ball of the foot and *not* the instep is placed on the pedal.

Saddle height should be adjusted to allow the ankle to drop at the top and be slightly extended at the bottom of the stroke, as shown (Fig. 4).

Body position is of great importance. An upright position is wasteful in effort and presents a large frontage to the wind. In Fig. 5a the weight of the rider is badly distributed and this is very tiring.

Fig. 5b shows the correct position where the angle of the body is at 45° to the horizontal and the arms at a similar angle. Here the weight is evenly distributed between saddle, handlebar and pedals.

For real speed a more streamlined position is necessary as shown in Fig. 5c. The racer "gets down to it." Pedalling efficiency is his first consideration and comfort takes second place. The weight is shared mainly between pedals and handlebar and the saddle is used mainly as a location.

Fig. 5

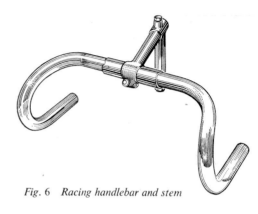

Fig. 6   Racing handlebar and stem

THE BICYCLE

Handlebars

The choice of a handlebar is a personal matter, but it should be chosen and adjusted to get the hands in the correct position. The average rider does not usually worry about this choice very much and is generally content with an "all-rounder" bar, where the grips are almost in a straight line with each other, and slightly raised above the centre. For the tourist it is useful to have a handlebar which provides a good position "on the tops" as well as a comfortable crouched lower stance. A speedman can use a deeper bar with an extension, but he normally adjusts the position with a long handlebar stem (Fig. 6).

Saddles

Leather has always been the most popular material for the saddle top and there are some mattress types of sprung seat with a leather or leather cloth top (Fig. 7a). However, some racing and sporting cyclists have now taken to the use of the nylon plastic saddle top (Fig. 7b), a material which is well suited to the job as it is not affected in any way by wet weather.

Most cyclists usually like a fairly wide saddle, but for speed, touring and racing a narrower type of saddle gives freer movement (Figs. 7c and 7d). Excessive springing in saddle design tends to lead to loss of pedalling efficiency and the simple steel framed saddle with resilient covering material, is normally best.

Leather saddles should be protected from bad weather because they tend to lose shape when used wet. All saddles have a tension screw in the nose but care should be taken not to overtighten this, or the moulded shape will be distorted.

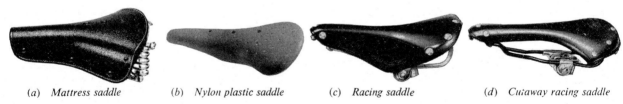

(a) *Mattress saddle*   (b) *Nylon plastic saddle*   (c) *Racing saddle*   (d) *Cutaway racing saddle*

Fig. 7   *Different types of saddle*

Frame design

Cycle frames may look alike but there are always some differences in each design. Angles and tube lengths vary according to the size of the machine; experience has decided these. The aim has always been a well-balanced bicycle.

Bicycle frame sizes are worked out by the length of the seat tube. The measurement, in inches, is taken from the centre of the bottom bracket axle to the top of the seat lug. This should be about 9 inches less than the rider's inside leg measurement. You can then easily adjust the saddle height by raising or lowering the pillar.

Don't assume that a larger frame is better. The horizontal top tube limits the extent to which you can adjust the handlebar height, so it is better to have a frame an inch smaller than too big. "Utility" cycles have wheel bases around 42 inches with a bracket height of 10½ inches from the ground. The racing cycle frequently has a wheel base reduced to 40 inches.

The weight of a cycle is most important and it should be kept as light as possible. A hand-built cycle frame "made to measure" by a specialist is naturally better than a factory bike but of course it costs more. Often these special frames have elaborately cut and fretted frame lugs. The small cycle builder is able to offer alternative angles, fork rakes, tube lengths and wheel bases to suit any customer.

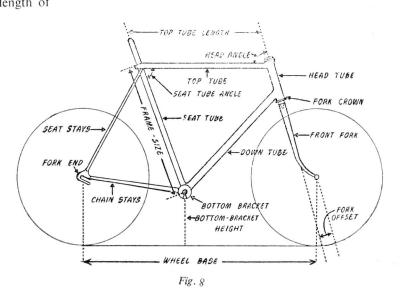

Fig. 8

Avoid extremes. A long wheel base may be more sluggish on hills yet provide better clearance for "derailleur" gears, as well as more comfort. A too-short machine can prove tricky to handle downhill and be unstable in the wet, but will seem to pick up the drive more readily.

Pedals

For everyday use, pedals usually have rubber treads (Fig. 9a), whereas the lightweight machines are fitted with the all-metal "rat-trap" pedal of which there are many different types (Figs. 9b and 9c).

Toeclips and straps (Fig. 10) help to make sure that the feet are correctly positioned on the pedals, and also

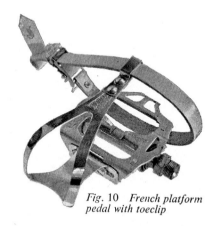

Fig. 10 *French platform pedal with toeclip*

(a) *Rubber tread pedal*

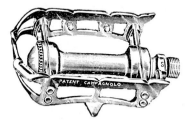

(b) *Road racing pedal*

(c) *Track racing pedal*

Fig. 9 *Different types of pedal*

assist the ankle action. With very little practice you will find that toeclips will much improve your pedalling efficiency. The straps should be adjusted to allow the foot to be pulled out quite easily.

Rat-trap pedals with toeclips are best used with special cycling shoes which have narrower soles than walking shoes.

Pedals need a little oil occasionally in order to keep the bearings running freely, and the cones should be adjusted if the pedal is either tight or has too much play.

To adjust, first remove the hexagon head end cap, slacken the lock nut and then use a screwdriver to move the cone in or out as required. Lock carefully again after adjustment.

It is a good idea to put a blob of grease in the dome of the hexagon headed cap before replacing it.

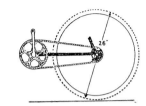

Fig. 11

Gearing

When the pedals are turned through a complete circle, the number of times the rear wheel rotates depends on the number of teeth on chain wheel and rear sprocket.

For example, if the chain wheel has 44 teeth on it and the rear sprocket 22 teeth (Fig. 11), then the back wheel will turn twice for every turn of the pedals. The bicycle would travel just as far as if the pedals were fixed directly on to a wheel twice the size. So, if the back wheel was 26 inches diameter, then every turn of the pedals would make the bicycle travel as far as an old "penny farthing" bicycle with a wheel twice as big, that is, 52 inches diameter (Fig. 12). This bicycle would then

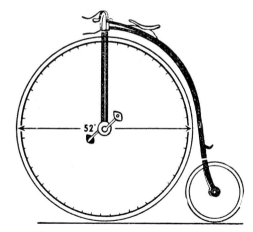

Fig. 12

be said to have a gear of 52 because gearing is still expressed by reference to the old "penny farthing" (see page 4). The formula for calculating the gear of a bicycle is:

$$\frac{\text{Number of teeth on chain wheel}}{\text{Number of teeth on rear sprocket}} \times \frac{\text{Wheel diameter in}}{\text{inches.}}$$

For most people a gear of about 65 is suitable but variable gears are very useful so that a change can be made when desired; lower gears when going uphill or against the wind and higher gears when conditions are easier.

Cycle chains

Utility or roadster cycles usually have 26 inch $\times$ 1$\frac{3}{8}$ inch wheels and have a chain with a standard pitch of $\frac{1}{2}$ inch and a width of $\frac{1}{8}$ inch. This chain is suitable for single geared cycles (or cycles with hub gears) and it is joined by a link which has a spring horseshoe clip to hold the link together. The closed end of the spring should point in the direction the chain normally moves, otherwise there is a danger of it being loosened if it catches on any external object.

Derailleur gears have a narrower chain, 3/32 inch wide and, as the clearances between sprockets are much more restricted, the chains are riveted together without the spring clip device. You should have a tool (Fig. 13) to extract the rivet from one of the links so that the chain can be removed and replaced

Keep the chain well-oiled with a light lubricant. Brush off mud and dirt to prevent excessive wear on the rollers.

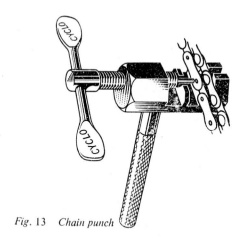

Fig. 13   Chain punch

When you fit a new derailleur chain, change the sprockets of the freewheel at the same time, because a new chain will not run satisfactorily on partly-worn sprockets. Wear on the chain wheel is not as heavy and any slight wear does not have the noisy effect that it has on the sprockets. However, the teeth should never be allowed to become hook-shaped.

Variable gearing

We have seen that the gear of a bicycle can be altered by changing the size of the rear sprocket or the chain wheel and this effect can be obtained by two different methods:

Gear table

Sprocket	38 26″	38 27″	40 26″	40 27″	42 26″	42 27″	44 26″	44 27″	46 26″	46 27″	47 26″	47 27″	48 26″	48 27″	49 26″	49 27″	50 26″	50 27″	51 26″	51 27″	52 26″	52 27″	53 26″	53 27″
12	82·4	85·5	86·7	90·0	91·0	94·5	95·3	99·0	99·7	103·5	101·8	105·7	104·0	108·0	106·1	110·2	108·3	112·5	110·5	114·7	112·7	117·0	114·8	119·3
13	76·0	78·9	80·0	83·1	84·0	87·2	88·0	91·4	92·0	95·5	94·0	97·6	96·0	99·7	98·0	101·8	100·0	103·9	102·0	105·9	104·0	108·0	106·0	110·0
14	70·6	73·3	74·3	77·1	78·0	81·0	81·7	84·9	85·4	88·7	87·3	90·6	89·1	92·6	91·0	94·5	92·9	96·4	94·7	98·3	96·6	100·3	98·4	102·2
15	65·9	68·4	69·3	72·0	72·8	75·6	76·3	79·2	79·7	82·8	81·5	84·6	83·2	86·4	84·9	88·2	86·7	90·0	88·4	91·8	90·1	93·6	91·8	95·4
16	61·8	64·1	65·0	67·5	68·3	70·9	71·5	74·3	74·6	77·6	76·4	79·3	78·0	81·0	79·6	82·7	81·3	84·4	82·9	86·0	84·5	87·8	86·1	89·4
17	58·1	60·3	61·2	63·5	64·2	66·7	67·3	69·9	70·4	73·1	71·9	74·6	73·4	76·2	74·9	77·8	76·5	79·4	78·0	81·0	79·5	82·6	81·0	84·1
18	54·9	57·0	57·8	60·0	60·6	63·0	63·6	66·0	66·4	69·0	67·9	70·5	69·3	72·0	70·7	73·5	72·2	75·0	73·6	76·5	75·1	78·0	76·5	79·5
19	52·0	54·0	54·7	56·8	57·5	59·7	60·2	62·5	62·9	65·4	64·3	66·8	65·7	68·2	67·0	69·6	68·4	71·1	69·8	72·4	71·2	73·9	72·5	75·3
20	49·4	51·3	52·0	54·0	54·6	56·7	57·2	59·4	59·8	62·1	61·1	63·4	62·4	64·8	63·7	66·2	65·0	67·5	66·3	68·5	67·6	70·2	68·9	71·5
21	47·1	48·9	49·5	51·4	52·0	54·0	54·5	56·6	57·0	59·1	68·2	60·4	59·4	61·7	60·6	63·0	61·9	64·3	63·1	65·5	64·4	66·9	65·6	68·1
22	44·9	46·6	47·3	49·1	49·6	51·5	52·0	54·0	54·4	56·5	55·5	57·6	56·7	58·9	57·9	60·1	59·1	61·4	60·2	62·5	61·5	63·8	62·6	65·0
23	43·0	44·6	45·2	47·0	47·5	49·3	49·8	51·6	52·0	54·0	53·1	55·2	54·3	56·3	55·4	57·5	56·5	58·7	57·6	59·8	58·8	61·0	59·9	62·2
24	41·2	41·8	43·3	45·0	45·5	47·3	47·7	49·5	49·9	51·8	50·9	52·9	52·0	54·0	53·1	55·1	54·2	56·3	55·2	57·3	56·3	58·5	57·4	59·6
25	39·5	41·0	41·6	43·2	43·7	45·4	45·8	47·5	47·8	49·7	48·9	50·8	49·9	51·8	51·0	52·9	52·0	54·0	53·0	55·8	54·1	56·2	55·1	57·2
26	38·0	39·5	40·0	41·5	42·0	43·6	44·0	45·7	46·0	47·8	47·0	48·8	49·0	49·9	49·0	50·9	51·0	51·9	51·0	53·7	52·0	54·0	53·0	55·0
28	35·3	36·6	37·1	38·6	39·0	40·5	40·9	42·4	42·7	44·4	43·6	45·3	44·6	46·3	45·5	47·2	46·4	48·2	47·3	49·8	48·3	50·1	49·2	51·1

(a) A hub gear which has enclosed within the rear wheel hub, an epicyclic gear mechanism with a chain of pinions (Fig. 14).

(b) The derailleur gear which has a mechanism enabling the chain to be moved from one sprocket to another as required (Fig. 15).

Hub gears

The standard is the 3-speed model which has a ratio of 3:4 between gears. Other models (no longer available) have been produced with different ratios in 3 and 4-gear varieties, the most recent development being a 5-speed hub with twin controls, but this is only obtainable to special order.

When the operating gear lever is in the "normal" position the sprocket and the rear wheel rotate together and the hub gear mechanism is not in use. Move the lever forward or backward and you get a higher or lower gear automatically. The hub needs only a little oil occasionally and is sealed from the weather. Take care when adjusting the wire connecting the operating lever so that the gears can be correctly engaged in the three positions.

Derailleur gears

These gears change the gear ratios by moving the chain from one sprocket on the back hub to another. The sprockets are mounted on a boss which screws on to the hub; the whole assembly is known as a "block" (Fig. 16) and usually has five different sprockets, giving five gear ratios, although it is possible to obtain a six-speed block. The derailleur gear principle can be used in conjunction with a 3-speed hub to give 6 or 9 gears, but care must be taken in the selection of sprocket sizes— 19/22 or 16/19/23 teeth will "match up" with the ratios inside the hub.

The most common way to obtain more than 5 gears, however, is to use a double chain wheel (Fig. 17), the inner chain ring having fewer teeth than the outer. The chain is moved from one chain ring to the other by a mechanism known as a front changer, which is mounted on the seat tube and controlled by a second lever.

The derailleur gear is a great help, but avoid keeping in high gear until you are forced to change down, also don't come to rest in high gear—you'll have to start off in it again, which places a strain on the bicycle and the rider. Try to use the lowest gear practicable (not the highest) so that your pedalling rate is not less than 60 to 70 revolutions per minute.

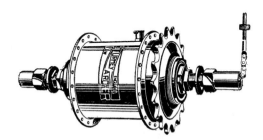

Fig. 14   Hub gear

A little oil on chain and rollers occasionally will keep things running smoothly but never oil the operating lever, which uses friction pressure plates to counteract the spring at the other end.

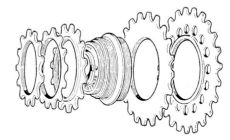

Fig. 16
Exploded view of block showing
how sprockets screw on to boss

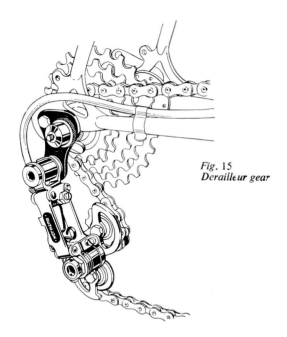

Fig. 15
Derailleur gear

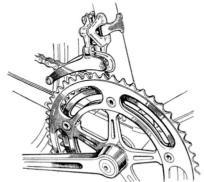

Fig. 17
Front changer and
double chain wheel

Wheels and tyres

As the wheels represent rolling weight the elimination of excess weight is necessary but care has to be taken to see that this is not overdone. Rigidity is also of importance so we need a combination of strength and lightness.

Rims are of two kinds: wired-on, which can be of either Endrick or Westwood shapes (Figs. 18a and 18b), and the sprint rim (Fig. 18c). The latter is designed for sporting use and is always used with tubular tyres, which are stuck on. Wired-on rims are the type we see most frequently. They are used with tyres that have wires woven into the fabric. This allows the outer cover to be removed easily so that the inner tube can be repaired when punctures occur. The principle used is a simple one but is not always understood. Wired-on rims have a step or shelf on either side. The wired edge of a tyre fits on this step snugly, the higher wall of the rim being sufficient to prevent the tyre blowing off.

The roadster tyre (Fig. 18d) is fitted with a robust, studded tread for utility work. For club cycling and touring, tyres with a combination of studs and ribs in the tread pattern (Fig. 18e) are most usual with the ribbed-only tread (Fig. 18f) reserved for speed work.

Tubular tyres (Fig. 18g) are cylindrical in section and have the inner tube encased in the outer covering which is sewn together at the base. With few exceptions, tubular tyres are light in weight, and have rather thin treads and consequently puncture rather easily. Repairs to tubular tyres involve the cutting of the stitches at the base of the tyre in order to extract the punctured portion of the inner tube and, of course, the re-stitching after repair.

The sprint rims for use with tubular tyres are almost flat and the tyres have to be stuck firmly to the rim with a special adhesive.

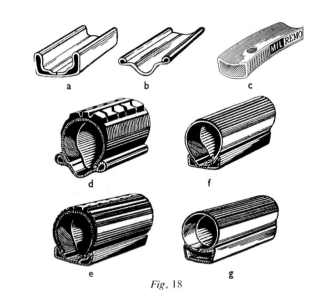

Fig. 18

Spokes

Unlike a cartwheel, a cycle wheel is held together by the tension applied to wire spokes. On utility cycles plain gauge spokes of 14 or 15 B.S. wire gauge suffice, but lightweight cycles use double-butted spokes which are 'drawn' so that they have the practical thickness of 14 or 15 gauge at both ends, the threaded end at the rim and the cranked head at the hub. The thickness of the spoke between these heavier ends is much less and is, of course, lighter.

Until recently it was normal for a front wheel to have 32 spokes and a rear wheel 40 spokes, but the Continental makers have long favoured 36 spokes in both wheels and this is now spreading to Britain. Some ultra-light racing wheels have been constructed with as few spokes as 28—or even 24.

Hubs

The wheel revolves on a spindle contained in the hub and this is usually secured in the forks of the cycle by means of two ordinary nuts.

In the case of road racing cycles, however, the wheel is held in place by a quick-release mechanism (Fig. 19) allowing the wheel to be removed by releasing a lever on the spindle. This facilitates wheel changing when punctures occur.

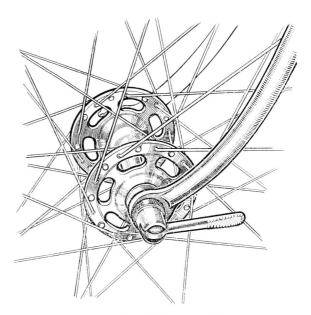

Fig. 19   Quick-release hub

Brakes

The law says that your bicycle must be fitted with an independent brake to each wheel.

Though many bicycles can still be seen with the pull-up, roller-lever brake system the principle has now largely been superseded by the cable-operated caliper brake. The old method used a series of cams and levers to transfer the pressure applied at the handlebar to the brake stirrups at the rim. This system worked best in conjunction with Westwood rims, a type of simple section and wide enough to allow the brake blocks to be applied from beneath.

The caliper brake (Fig. 20a), used in conjunction with an Endrick (flat-sided) rim has been continually improved and there is now a wide choice. Caliper brakes are frequently of light alloy construction. At one time cable brakes had a bad reputation of being rather one-sided in action and leaving one brake block still in contact with the rim. Though modern side-pulls have reduced this fault, the defect has resulted in the introduction of

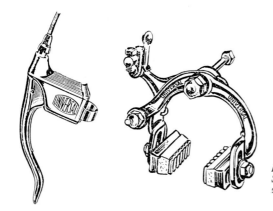

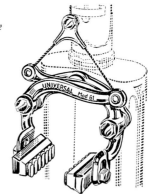

Fig. 20b
Centre-pull brake

Fig. 20a
Side-pull caliper brake
and typical brake lever

a wide range of centre pull brakes (Figs. 20b and 20c) which have an independent spring on either side. The centre-pull seems to gain in popularity but the cables on the side-pull type are more conveniently placed alongside the frame of the cycle.

Two other types of cycle brakes must be mentioned. The hub brake (Fig. 20d), a scaled down version of the car brake, has a pair of semi-circular shoes, fitted with a hard fibrous lining, which operate internally on the drum-like shell of the hub.

It is rarely used today, however, for although of high efficiency when new, the linings tend to absorb oil which make the brake ineffective. The heavier weight of this type is also against the trend to make the bicycle lighter with each scientific advance.

One of the most efficient rear brakes, the "coaster hub" (generally known as the back-pedal brake) is seen only occasionally, though it deserves wider popularity. It is used on some of the modern 20 inch wheel folding bicycles which can be stowed away in a car boot—here the absence of a rear brake cable is an advantage.

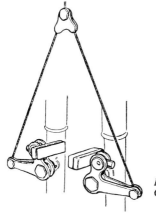

Fig. 20c
Centre-pull brake

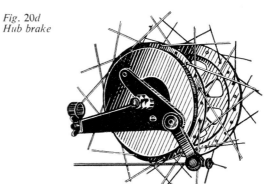

Fig. 20d
Hub brake

Brakes in use

In normal circumstances brakes should be applied gently. Do not snatch at the lever but pull steadily, increasing the pressure gradually. Emergency braking is used when you have not had a chance to plan the move ahead.

Most cyclists like to have the rear brake lever on the left-hand side of the handlebar, enabling the important right-hand signals to be given while speed is controlled with the rear brake.

A front brake is usually more effective in stopping a cycle than is the rear brake, but should always be applied carefully.

When brakes are fully "on", brake levers should not be touching or nearly touching the handlebar. If they are, then fit new brake blocks or adjust the brakes at once.

When in good condition cycle brakes are very effective but there are times when this efficiency can be a disadvantage. On a slippery surface, wet roads, mud, leaf strewn roads and loose gravel, braking must be done with extreme caution. If you apply brakes when turning under these conditions the wheels may slip from under you and you may find yourself lying on the ground possibly in the path of a motor car. Learn to anticipate these problems and avoid sharp turns on wet roads or loose grit.

Even when riding straight but downhill, caution is required, for harsh or sudden braking will lock the wheels and an uncontrollable slide is the result. In all kinds of weather but especially when it is wet, the skilful cyclist makes sure that he will not have to put his brakes on suddenly for anything that he ought to have foreseen.

The expert makes a practice of applying his brakes lightly at the top of every hill to ensure that they are working properly and ready for action when he needs them. During rain and on wet roads the film of water on the rims delays brake action and some distance is covered before the full retarding effect of the brake action is felt.

In wet conditions it is a good idea to apply the brakes from time to time, to help to dry the rims.

Chain set

The majority of chain sets are made of steel and the cranks are secured to the bottom bracket spindle by cotter pins. With the trend towards less weight, and despite their higher price, light alloy cranks (Fig. 21) are becoming increasingly popular, especially with racing cyclists.

Because of the softness of the alloy, cotter pins cannot be used so the cranks are bolted on to the spindle.

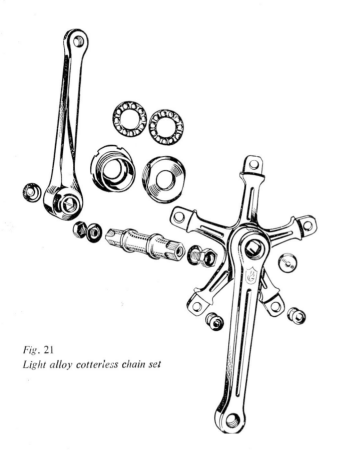

Fig. 21
Light alloy cotterless chain set

CARRYING LUGGAGE

If you have a parcel or a bag to carry do not let it dangle from the handlebar where it may entangle with the front wheel and will certainly affect the steering. Neither is it a good practice to carry luggage in a haversack or kit-bag slung across the shoulders. Carry luggage in the proper place in a saddlebag (Fig. 22) or on a luggage carrier.

Fig. 22   *Saddle Bag*

Holiday luggage is best managed with pannier bags (Fig. 23) astride the rear wheel, but ensure that the carrier you use to support them is really strong and rigid. The carrier should not move at all from side to side. A load which wobbles out of rhythm with the bicycle because of a poorly fastened or too "whippy" carrier is a menace to safety.

Tourists often use front pannier bags, or a handlebar bag, to carry extra luggage but these should be quite small and restricted to the carrying of light articles.

When packing your luggage remember to leave your cape in an easily accessible position—on straps outside the saddle bag is best—and keep your maps handy too.

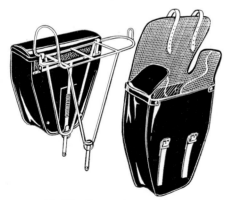

Fig. 23   Pannier bags and carrier

LIGHTING

There are strict legal rules about lighting (see page 30).

Electric battery lamps are very convenient and have the advantage of being easily removable when not in use. However, it is wise to carry a spare battery and bulbs in your saddlebag in case of failure. A partly used battery may seem to provide a usable light when first switched on but can deteriorate rapidly and give only a dim light later. Always remove the battery from the lamp before putting it away during the summer, otherwise the acid may leak and destroy the inside metalwork of the lamp.

Dynamo lighting provides more light, is probably cheaper in the long run, and there is not the bother of having to renew batteries frequently. A popular style comprises a front lamp, a rear lamp and a small generator which applies a roller to the tread of the tyre and can be used on either wheel. The rear bulb must be at least 6 volt .1 amp.

Dynamos (also called generators) which are operated by the tyre demand special care in fitting (Fig. 25). The axis of the dynamo (the centre line of its revolving shaft) *MUST* be in line with the radius of the wheel. Even a slight error of angle will result in excessive noise and rapid wear of both tyre and generator bearings. The height on the forks is also of great importance, for the roller should be placed so that the curve of the tyre is central. If it is too low or too high, the edge of the roller will cut a groove in the tyre wall.

Fig. 24
Battery rear lamp

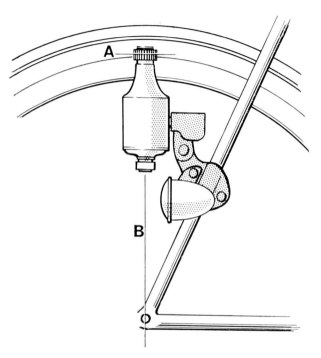

Fig. 25 *The dynamo roller should make contact with the tyre about half way up the wall (A). The axis of the dynamo should be in line with the radius of the wheel (B)*

Fig. 26   Hub dynamo

The dynohub (Fig. 26), a lighting set where the generator is part of one of the hubs, is comparatively trouble free and provides adequate lighting. However, if you ever have occasion to dismantle the hub to attend to the bearings do not allow the magnet and the rotor to separate *even for an instant*. The dynohub uses a compound magnetic field which breaks down if these two parts are not kept one within the other. Treat them as one unit and replace both if you have any trouble. Weight is a possible disadvantage but is not one that worries the utility rider.

Every cycle must, by law, be equipped with an efficient and approved reflector, but see that it is kept clean. Develop the habit of giving the face of both reflector and rear lamp a quick rub whenever you wheel your machine out to the road.

BICYCLE MAINTENANCE
Bearings and adjustment

A bicycle is easily maintained though so often neglected. Ease of running and long life of wearing parts depend on occasional attention to main bearings. The wheel hubs, bottom bracket, steering head, pedals and gear mechanisms are all equipped with ball bearings which have adjustment facilities that need periodic attention. These are designed to run freely with as little side play as possible. Pedals, hubs, bottom brackets (Fig. 27) and the rollers of derailleurs all use a simple principle which is easily understood.

The steering head (Fig. 28) uses the same principle but because the load is disposed in a different manner it is more difficult to decide when it should need attention. Unfortunately the headset will work well when "slack" but this permits road vibrations to hammer the hard steel ball bearings into the lower races. As head bearings do not continually rotate, the hammering effect is always in the same spot and the bearing surfaces are ruined. The answer is that one should keep the head set properly adjusted at all times; free, but without play.

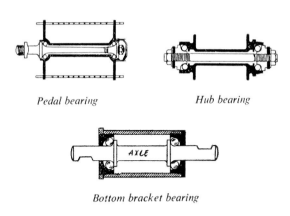

Pedal bearing　　　　　*Hub bearing*

AXLE

Bottom bracket bearing

Fig. 27

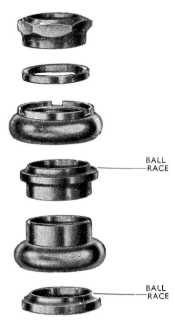

BALL RACE

BALL RACE

Fig. 28　Head set assembly

Lubrication

A bicycle needs little oil but it needs it frequently. Excessive oil can be as harmful as too little. Wherever two pieces of metal move against each other the movement will be assisted by lubrication and rust is also prevented. Whenever you fit a new brake cable or a gear wire, grease the wire before inserting it in the outer casing but always ensure that oil or grease does not get on to the brake blocks or wheel rims.

Care of your cycle

Every time you take your cycle out make the following check:—

See that the tyres are really hard. If they are soft—if you can squeeze them in when pressing with the thumb and forefinger at the sides—they will wear out more quickly and will be more sluggish to ride on.

Check the play in the front and rear wheels. If necessary make the appropriate adjustments.

Make sure that the brakes are working properly.

See that the repair outfit and pump are where they should be—on the bicycle, and not left behind in the cycle shed.

If you are going to be out after dark, make sure your lamps are in good order.

Remember to take your cape or other waterproof.

How to mend a puncture

Turn the bicycle upside down (remember to protect the top of the saddle and the handlebars from the rough surface of the ground) and work from the side opposite to the chain. If the position of the puncture is known, it may not be necessary to remove *all* the tyre. Insert three tyre levers, one after the other between the wire of the outer cover and the rim of the wheel; lever the appropriate section of the outer cover off the rim and pull out sufficient length of the inner tube to enable you to attend to the puncture.

If the position of the puncture is not known, it may be necessary to search for it by passing the tube through a bowl of water, so that escaping air will cause bubbles. Mark the place with indelible pencil or ink. This procedure will of course mean taking the wheel out completely and removing the inner tube from the outer cover.

Clean around the puncture with sandpaper, scraper or sulphur stick contained in the repair outfit. Select a patch of a size to allow about half an inch to project all round the hole in the tube. Smear the cleaned area with rubber solution and *allow to become almost dry*. Then remove the patch from its protective linen or silver foil and press the patch into position on the tube. Use the thumbs of both hands to make sure that the edges of the patch are brought into firm contact with the tube. In a few moments the patch will have adhered sufficiently for the tube to be replaced, but before that is done the cover should be examined both inside and out to see if the nail or stone that caused the puncture is still embedded in the tyre. Take this opportunity of removing any grit inside the outer cover, and dust the inside of the cover with french chalk before inserting the tube.

When the patch is firm and the tyre has been examined for any other damage, replace the inner tube inside the cover, making sure that the valve is properly positioned in the hole in the rim. Then give the inner tube two or three pumps of air: this will allow the tube to be tucked neatly into the cover, and the cover pulled evenly up to the rim ready for putting back on. The cover should be pushed back on to the rim with the hands, using mainly the thumbs. Tyre levers should not be used for this purpose because there is a danger of pinching the tube between the rim and the tyre lever. Make sure that the tube has not been pinched between the edge of the cover and the rim and that the valve is seated properly and not pulled sideways, then inflate the tyre hard.

Fig. 29   A roadside puncture repair

Keep your bicycle in good order

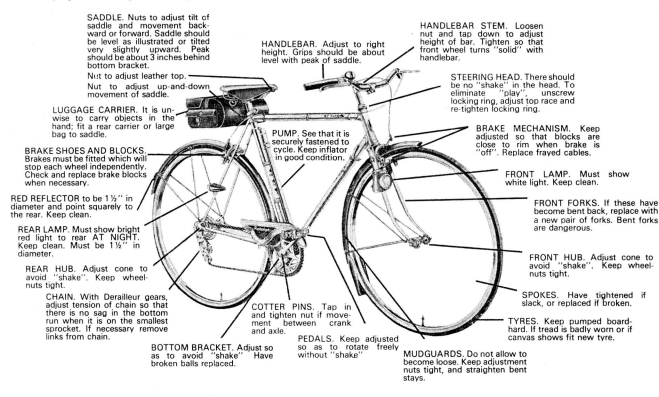

SADDLE. Nuts to adjust tilt of saddle and movement backward or forward. Saddle should be level as illustrated or tilted very slightly upward. Peak should be about 3 inches behind bottom bracket.

Nut to adjust leather top.

Nut to adjust up-and-down movement of saddle.

LUGGAGE CARRIER. It is unwise to carry objects in the hand; fit a rear carrier or large bag to saddle.

BRAKE SHOES AND BLOCKS. Brakes must be fitted which will stop each wheel independently. Check and replace brake blocks when necessary.

RED REFLECTOR to be 1½'' in diameter and point squarely to the rear. Keep clean.

REAR LAMP. Must show bright red light to rear AT NIGHT. Keep clean. Must be 1½'' in diameter.

REAR HUB. Adjust cone to avoid ''shake''. Keep wheel-nuts tight.

CHAIN. With Derailleur gears, adjust tension of chain so that there is no sag in the bottom run when it is on the smallest sprocket. If necessary remove links from chain.

BOTTOM BRACKET. Adjust so as to avoid ''shake'' Have broken balls replaced.

HANDLEBAR. Adjust to right height. Grips should be about level with peak of saddle.

PUMP. See that it is securely fastened to cycle. Keep inflator in good condition.

COTTER PINS. Tap in and tighten nut if movement between crank and axle.

PEDALS. Keep adjusted so as to rotate freely without ''shake''

HANDLEBAR STEM. Loosen nut and tap down to adjust height of bar. Tighten so that front wheel turns ''solid'' with handlebar.

STEERING HEAD. There should be no ''shake'' in the head. To eliminate ''play'', unscrew locking ring, adjust top race and re-tighten locking ring.

BRAKE MECHANISM. Keep adjusted so that blocks are close to rim when brake is ''off''. Replace frayed cables.

FRONT LAMP. Must show white light. Keep clean.

FRONT FORKS. If these have become bent back, replace with a new pair of forks. Bent forks are dangerous.

FRONT HUB. Adjust cone to avoid ''shake''. Keep wheel-nuts tight.

SPOKES. Have tightened if slack, or replaced if broken.

TYRES. Keep pumped board-hard. If tread is badly worn or if canvas shows fit new tyre.

MUDGUARDS. Do not allow to become loose. Keep adjustment nuts tight, and straighten bent stays.

SKILFUL CYCLING

Every cyclist should be fully conversant with the laws that govern the use of the road, and with the Highway Code.

A "stop" sign must be observed by cyclists. You are expected to stop and place one foot on the ground before proceeding into a major road after seeing that the way is clear.

You must give way to people using pedestrian crossings, and must always obey police signals, traffic lights and traffic signs.

When you are going to change direction, or to slow down or stop, you must think of the effect that your action may have on other road users. You must give ample and timely warning of your intentions in a clear manner that cannot be misunderstood.

Turning to the right. A frequent cause of complaint against cyclists is inadequate signalling of intention to make a turn to the right. And indeed this is a manoeuvre of the utmost importance, and one which from a safety point of view requires the rider's fullest attention and skill.

When you wish to enter a road which is on your right, it is essential first of all to look over your shoulder to ascertain what traffic is coming up behind you. This should be done well in advance of the road junction. When you are sure that there is a sufficient gap between you and the vehicles behind, give the right hand signal clearly and unmistakably and move out towards the

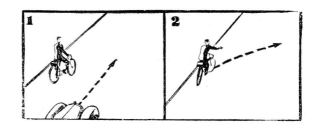

Fig. 30   *The correct way to turn right*

centre of the road. Do not be diffident about your signal; put your arm out to its fullest extent, straight from the shoulder.

Having reached the middle of the road, remain there and continue riding until you are opposite the right hand turn, keeping your right arm out all the time. Overtaking traffic will now be passing you on your left. If traffic coming towards you prevents you making the right hand turn immediately, stop in the centre of the road opposite the junction and wait for a break in the traffic. When there is a break, ride into the turning, still signalling if necessary. Do not cut the corner but keep well to the left and leave room for traffic coming out of the turning.

The Highway Code includes some special rules for cyclists only, such as:—

If there is an adequate cycle path beside the road, ride on it;

Do not ride more than two abreast. Ride in single file on busy or narrow roads;

Do not carry anything which may affect your balance;

Do not hold on to another vehicle or another cyclist;

Do not ride close behind another vehicle.

The Law Demands

That your cycle has efficient brakes;

That after the official "hours of darkness" a white front light must be shown forward and be bright enough to be seen from a "reasonable distance." In addition, a red rear light marked with British Standard 3648 and a reflector (B.S.2515) must be fitted. Both the rear light lens and the reflector must be over $1\frac{1}{2}$ inches in diameter;

That you must observe traffic signs and signals or policeman's directions EVEN IF YOU ARE WHEELING YOUR CYCLE;

That you must stop if signalled to do so by a school patrol.

You Must Not:—

Ride recklessly or in a manner dangerous to the public;

Ride without due care and attention or without reasonable consideration for other persons on the road;

Ride under the influence of drink or a drug;

Ride on a footway made or set apart for the use of pedestrians;

Carry a passenger on a bicycle not constructed or adapted to carry more than one person;

Hold on to a motor vehicle or trailer in motion on any road.

The National Cycling Proficiency Scheme

Riding a bicycle should be easy, comfortable and safe. A skilful cyclist enjoys the adventure that his machine can give, but the bike-rider calls it a "push-bike" probably because he spends most of his energy doing just that!

Nowadays, cycling by young people plays an important part in their development as safe and proficient road users of the future.

Ideally everyone should serve a 'road apprenticeship' as a cyclist to learn road sense and speed judgment before attempting to learn how to drive a motor vehicle.

Many of the casualties on our roads are caused by ignorance of road laws, incorrect or slipshod signalling, lack of understanding of the machines being driven or just plain thoughtlessness.

The importance of proper training by experts cannot be over-emphasised, and the National Cycling Proficiency Scheme provides both facilities and skilled instructors. The scheme is sponsored by the Department of the Environment and administered with the help of local authorities, by RoSPA (The Royal Society for the Prevention of Accidents). It is carefully designed to encourage young cyclists to attain proficiency in road sense, cycling skill, and knowledge of the Highway Code. Candidates who are successful in the national test are awarded the National Cycling Proficiency Certificate and Badge. Information may be obtained from local road safety officers, the police, headmasters in schools or from RoSPA, Royal Oak Centre, Brighton Road, Purley CR2 2UR.

Cycle shops showing the National Proficiency sign, a red triangle on a blue circular background, may also be able to supply information about local facilities. The National Cycling Proficiency Test may be undertaken only after an adequate course of instruction.

Fig. 31   *A child being tested in bicycle control—part of the National Cycling Proficiency Test*

CYCLING CLUBS

To get the best out of cycling you should become a member of a cycling club, for club life is a great joy. It gives the cyclist the experience so essential to confident and skilful use of his machine, and opens the way to wider enjoyment of the pastime. Every district has its local club or clubs providing riding and social facilities for their members, and some clubs specialise in touring club runs and organise visits to places of interest. Prominent among these are the local sections of the Cyclists' Touring Club who offer an all the year round programme of such runs every weekend, as well as holiday tours and social events throughout the winter.

This activity, however, is only part of the wide range of services offered to its members by the Cyclists' Touring Club, a national organisation founded as long ago as 1878. As well as providing local activity through its district associations and sections, the C.T.C. is prominent in the defence of cyclists' rights to use the public roads and also for such benefits of membership as free legal aid, third party insurance, special insurances for cycles and their riders, touring routes and travel bureau services, club magazine, etc. It also organises national events such as the annual York Rally, and special Adventure Weeks for young cyclists.

Most individual cycling clubs are affiliated to the British Cycling Federation. The B.C.F. is concerned mainly with the administration of the sport of road and track racing, but it also provides a range of services to members similar to those of the C.T.C.

GROUP RIDING

It is very pleasant indeed to ride merrily along the roads and lanes of Britain in company of one or more companions. There are, in fact, few aspects of cycling to compare with it for sheer enjoyment, and riders who share their pleasures in that way usually find that they can ride further than when they are alone. The lone cyclist, unless he is very experienced, often tires more quickly than one in a group.

Group riding carries with it certain duties and obligations. It is not just riding in a bunch. In the first place, every member of the group must remember the safety and convenience of the other riders; he must keep a reasonable distance behind the back wheel of the rider in front and he must not make sudden changes of direction or speed without warning, or he may cause difficulties to the rider behind.

When riding on the outside always remember to leave the inner rider room to manoeuvre to negotiate a pot-hole or some other obstacle, and not to squeeze him into the side of the road.

The leader of a group, whether it is an actual part of a cycling club or merely a number of friends who have joined together for an impromptu excursion, should ride in front and should be actually in charge of the rest of the party. When he wishes the group to come to a halt he should call a word of warning to those behind him and allow a few seconds before actually applying his brakes. At the back of the party there should be a "second in command" to give warning when other vehicles wish to overtake. A large group of cyclists should be broken up so that overtaking for faster vehicles is simplified.

If two cyclists are riding together side by side and it is necessary to fall into single file, it is usual for the one on the *inside* to go *forward* and the one on the *outside* to fall *behind*.

CYCLE TOURING

Although, as we have seen, the bicycle has now been with us for over a hundred years, there are still many thousands of people who have never discovered the delights it has to offer and, indeed, who cannot understand why anybody should wish to indulge in such "hard work" as a means of getting about. This attitude is, of course, not improved by the increasing use and ownership of motor vehicles in our modern age.

The enthusiastic cycle tourist, however, can readily supply the answer, for he or she knows that the pedal cycle is the perfect medium for touring and recreational travel. Less restrictive and less tiring than walking, the bicycle still affords the essential delight of travelling silently through the chosen scene at a pace which allows the rider to enjoy to the full the sights, sounds and scents of the countryside around him. His is not a view of the landscape glimpsed through a window at speed, nor a quick breath of fresh air at the journey's end; his pleasures are with him all the time he travels along.

Of course, if cycle touring is to be enjoyed fully it must be practised properly, and the rules and advice given elsewhere in this book with regard to such things as pedalling and riding position, gearing and luggage carrying, must be observed. Whether enjoying just a day's run, a weekend away or a full touring holiday lasting several weeks, the cycle tourist must learn to ride within the limit of his capabilities and to remember that ease, comfort and enjoyment of the ride are more important than sheer speed or distance. If this is not remembered then the tour will become the "hard work" that the critics always say it is.

Touring in its fullest sense means riding under all sorts of conditions and over all kinds of terrain, and gearing is therefore of considerable importance. For easy hill climbing, the bicycle must have a gear range capable of giving a low gear of about 40, and even lower if the tour is through very mountainous districts. Properly equipped cyclists can, and do, ride all the way through the Alps, and to free-wheel down the other side is an experience beyond compare.

Going abroad for a cycling holiday is not so difficult now as it used to be, and there are only a few formalities. Nevertheless some cyclists still like to have the guidance of experienced hands on their first tour in foreign lands, and for this purpose the Cyclists' Touring Club organises a series of such tours each year, with fully qualified leaders. Parties are usually about sixteen strong and the countries visited include such superb touring grounds as France, Italy, Spain, Austria, Norway (Fig. 32), Corsica, Switzerland and Iceland.

Fig. 32   Members of the C.T.C. touring in Norway

Competition for cycle tourists

Although touring is not usually associated directly with the competitive side of the cycling game, an event is well established on the cyclists' calendar which provides an outlet for competition among the tourists. Organised by the C.T.C., the British Cycle Tourist Competition was introduced in 1952 and has since gone from strength to strength as a national event. The Competition seeks to find Britain's best all round cycle tourist every year, and is an intensive test of skill in such matters as map reading, touring and countryside knowledge, road conduct and courtesy, observation and route following. The Competition is organised first by the C.T.C's district associations in heats all over the country during April, May and June and those qualifying from the heats ride later in the year in a National Final in a specially chosen area. Trophies are awarded to the outright winner, and to the most successful lady and junior competitors.

CYCLE SPORT

Cycle racing in one form or another provides one of the most satisfying outlets for youthful energy and the natural desire to do better than the other fellow. There are organised races and trials throughout the year and there are special events when a novice can try his skill alongside others who are also newcomers.

When a cyclist has developed confidence he will tend to become more ambitious. He finds himself travelling farther afield and with more ease and soon is imbued with the competitive spirit as he begins to catch up another rider that he has seen in the distance. This is but a step away from the fascinating sport of time trialing where a rider can assess his own prowess "against the watch" on accurately measured stretches of road.

Time trialing

The sport is controlled by the Road Time Trials Council in such a manner as to ensure that there is not the slightest hindrance to other road users. The cycling club organising the event will recruit a number of its members to act as course marshals (Fig. 33) whose duty it is to stand at various points on the course, such as cross-roads and roundabouts, where competitors may possibly encounter hazards. The marshals will warn them of the approach of traffic and also indicate the route to be taken. Each rider is allotted a starting time (the very early hours of the morning are most usual) and is despatched to ride alone over a measured course, eventually being timed in by an official at the finish. The period of time taken by the rider to cover the distance is worked out and the finishing list made up in the order of the fastest ones first.

Handicaps to encourage the newcomer and team races to foster inter-club rivalry are incorporated in the events which may be 10, 25, 50 or 100 miles in length, while in summer and autumn there are trials at both 12 hours and 24 hours, the object being for the rider to travel the greatest distance possible in the allotted time.

The essential feature of this exhilarating sport is the fact that every rider must ride alone and unpaced. Thus if he is overtaken by another rider, or catches one himself, he must not give chase nor ride in company with the other cyclist. Although in essence this is a race, every rider has the satisfaction of achieving an individual time for the distance, and even the slowest ones enjoy the continual urge to beat their previous best time for the distance.

Fig. 33 Marshals direct a rider in an early morning time trial J. B. Wadley

The cycles used in time trialing vary greatly depending on the length and type of course, but the rider's aim, as in all branches of the sport, is to have a machine that is as light and responsive as possible.

This does not mean, however, that a beginner needs a great sum of money to obtain a suitable machine. Most good lightweight cycle builders produce excellent frame sets or even complete cycles at comparatively low prices which provide the novice with a good, all-round mount quite suitable for general club riding and massed start racing as well as time trialing.

Fig. 34   Track racing at Herne Hill, London

Sporting Cyclist

Track racing

Exceptionally thrilling and probably one of the liveliest sports to watch is track racing. There are a number of towns which possess tracks where this sport can be seen and among these are Herne Hill and Paddington (London), Leicester, Edinburgh, Cardiff, Kirkby (Liverpool) and Nottingham. Riders at these tracks display the great skill, style and tactics that make the sport so varied and exciting.

Unlike time trialing, the riders start together and are in direct competition. The events are held on smooth, banked circuits. The older tracks are mostly about 400 metres long but the modern track at Leicester is 333.33 metres. The cycles used in such competitions differ from those used in road racing as they have no brakes, no gears and are different in frame design, having a shorter wheelbase and special rear fork ends; this prevents the back wheel being pulled out of the forks when riders exert a sudden terrific force on the chain when sprinting and permits the use of chain adjusters.

A variation on the normal track race is the pursuit race. One rider starts off exactly half way round the track ahead of the other, the object being for each rider to try to lessen the distance from the other over a certain number of laps. The winner is the man who has made up the most ground.

There are also many smaller events throughout the country held on grass tracks. These tracks are exactly the same as those used for athletics and often one track is used for both sports.

The cycles used on this type of track are exactly the same as those used on the asphalt type, apart from the tubular tyres, which have a "knobbly" tread and are heavier than the silk variety used in normal track racing.

Road racing

Road racing, a sport controlled in this country by the British Cycling Federation, has gained great popularity and British riders now compete successfully with the

Fig. 35 *Competitors in the Tour of Britain road race riding through the New Forest*

Fig. 36 Massed start riders tackling a steep gradient.

champions from the continent where cycling is the national sport.

Competitors start together in one group (usually limited to forty), hence the name frequently used to describe this sport "massed start." This illustrates the principal difference between road racing and time trialing. Time ceases to be of paramount importance and exact distance does not matter, for the winner is the first rider to cross the finishing line at the end.

The courses used are more arduous than those used

by the time trialist, for difficult terrain, steep hills (Fig. 36) and tricky descents help to sort out the riders. Even the toughest course is not always enough to permit the better riders to escape from the main group, though they try constantly, and often the ultimate winner is decided by a burst of speed in the last few yards with many riders still close behind. Courses are arranged with a view to avoiding inconvenience to other road users as much as possible. Roads through built-up areas are unsuitable and many courses take the form of circuits around safe but hilly routes, even covering the circuit many times before the finish which is at a wide stretch of road usually where spectators can watch the thrilling finish without having to stand in the roadway. Races can vary from a short criterium of about 10 miles on a closed circuit up to a distance of 150 miles, with the majority of events being held over 80-100 miles.

Road racing—affiliation and licences

Cyclists who wish to race must first join the British Cycling Federation. A racing man's skill is shown by the licence that he is permitted to hold. B.C.F. members start with a 3rd category licence from which they have to win promotion to the 2nd category and eventually by further successes to the 1st category. The licensing system enables events to be graded so that riders are able to compete with others of similar ability.

Schoolboys' Championships

The British Cycling Federation runs National Schoolboys' Championships each year. Heats for the National Road Championship are held by local B.C.F. divisions with the final being held in a different area each year.

Sprint and Pursuit Championships are also held each year.

Entrants for both championships must be over 14 years of age and under 16 on the day of the Division heat, and must be members of the British Cycling Federation.

More detailed information on the subject of racing is contained in the companion volume **KTG Cycle Racing.**

Printed in Great Britain by Elsworth Bros. Ltd , Leeds.